# Chi-obaa and Her Town

I Talk You Talk Press

Copyright © 2018 I Talk You Talk Press

ISBN: 978-4-907056-99-5

www.italkyoutalk.com

info@italkyoutalk.com

All rights reserved. No part of this publication may be resold, reproduced, stored in retrieval system, copied in any form or by any means, electronic, mechanical, photocopying, recording or otherwise transmitted without the prior written permission from the publisher. You must not circulate this publication in any format, online or otherwise.

This is a work of fiction. Names, characters, businesses, organizations, products, places, events and incidents are either the products of the author's imagination or are used in a fictitious manner. We have no affiliation with any existing companies mentioned in this story. Any resemblance to actual persons, living or dead, existing stories or actual events is purely coincidental.

Although the author and publisher have made every effort to ensure that the contents of this book were correct at press time, the author and publisher do not assume and hereby disclaim any liability to any party for any loss, damage, or disruption caused by errors or omissions, whether such errors or omissions result from negligence, accident, or any other cause.

For more information, see the Copyright Notice on our website.

Image copyright: © Paylessimages #17343792 Standard License

## CONTENTS

Introduction – Meet Chi-obaa     1

### CHI-OBAA AND THE GOVERNOR

1. Monday morning     5

2. Monday afternoon     9

3. Monday night     13

4. Tuesday     15

5. Wednesday     19

6. Thursday     22

### CHI-OBAA AND THE TRICYCLE

1. A present for Hatsuko     27

2. What did you see and hear?     30

3. The tricycle thief     34

4. Sho     40

5. The fish man        43

Thank You              47

About the Author       48

# INTRODUCTION

## MEET CHI-OBAA

These are stories about Chi-obaa, her family and her friends. Chi-obaa has an interesting life. Before you read about Chi-obaa's adventures, I would like you to meet her. You might like to meet her friends and family too.

Mameko Saito lives in Nakashige-cho with her eldest son and his wife. She has three grandchildren.
But no one calls her 'Mameko'. Everyone calls Mameko 'Chi-obaa'. 'Chi-obaa' is short for 'chiisai obaa-san'. 'Chiisai obaa-san' means 'little grandmother' in Japanese.
Her children and grandchildren call her Chi-obaa too. The only person who doesn't call her Chi-obaa, is her daughter-in-law, Kaneko. Kaneko calls her 'okaa-san'. 'Okaa-san' means 'mother' in Japanese.
Chi-obaa is very small. She is 79 years old. Every year she gets smaller, but her energy seems to grow. She is always busy and she is always smiling. Chi-obaa likes bright colours, such as red, pink and purple. Her clothes are very colourful.
Chi-obaa's life was very hard. She was an only child, but when she was 12 years old, her family sent her away from Nakashige-cho. She was sent to Osaka to work in a boarding house. She had to cook and clean for the guests all day. She sent all the money she earned back to her family in Nakashige-cho. When she was 28 years old, she married a man who lived in the boarding house. They had two children. When Chi-obaa was 32 years old, her husband died. Her children were very young. Chi-obaa had no money, so she went back to Nakashige-cho with her children. She cared for her parents, grew

vegetables and looked after her children. She worked 16 hours every day. After a few years, her parents died. When Chi-obaa's son was in high school, Chi-obaa sold the land around her house. She wanted money so that her son could go to university. Then she worked as a cleaner for many years.

When Chi-obaa was 65 years old, her son married. He got a good job in the government offices in the city near Nakashige-cho. After he married, he and his wife moved back to his mother's house. When they moved back, Chi-obaa said, "At last! Now I can retire! I've been working for other people all my life. Now I will do everything I want to do for myself."

Chi-obaa has three very important possessions. Her mobile phone, the ipod-nano her grandson gave her when he got an itouch, and her shopping walker. A shopping walker is a bag or box on wheels. Chi-obaa's shopping walker is special. She can carry many things in her walker. It has four wheels, a seat and a brake. Chi-obaa can take a rest anytime by sitting on the walker.

Would you like to meet Chi-obaa's friends and family?

Chi-obaa has two very good friends, Hatsuko and Hanae. They have known each other since they were in primary school.

Hatsuko Nakamura is 79 years old. She married the owner of the barber's shop in Nakashige-cho when she was 22 years old. Hatsuko spent all her life working in the barber's shop. They had three children. One child died when he was very young. When Hatsuko's husband died, her son, Taihei, changed the barber's shop into a fashionable hair salon.

Hatsuko is very tall and thin, and she always wears a hat. She is famous in Nakashige-cho because she is the neighbourhood tama-ire champion. Tama-ire is a competition where teams throw small beanbags into a basket. The basket is on a pole about four metres above the ground. The team with the most goals wins the competition. The towns around Nakashige-cho have a community sports day once a year. All the residents take part in different sporting events. Thanks to Hatsuko, Nakashige-cho always wins the tama-ire competition.

Hanae Yamamoto says she is 70 years old. Chi-obaa and Hatsuko know she is really 78 but they don't say anything. Hanae grew up in

Nakashige-cho, but she moved to Tokyo when she was young. Her mother died and her father left Nakashige-cho and moved to Kyushu, in southern Japan. No one heard anything about Hanae for many years. Then suddenly after more than forty years, Hanae came back to Nakashige-cho. She bought an expensive place in a new apartment block. She seems to have a lot of money. Her clothes are very expensive and she goes to the hairdresser every week, so her hair is always black. She never talks about her years in Tokyo. Chi-obaa and Hatsuko know Hanae has a secret, but they do not ask her questions.

Kenshin Saito is Chi-obaa's eldest son. He works in the local government office. He is a quiet man. People in Nakashige-cho often call him 'Chi-obaa-no-musuko'. This means 'Chi-obaa's son'. Kaneko doesn't like this.

Kaneko is Kenshin's wife. Kaneko and Kenshin met at university in Okayama City. Okayama is Kaneko's hometown. She is a very nice woman and is a good wife and mother. However, her life is difficult because Chi-obaa lives with them. Kaneko cannot understand her mother-in-law. She would like a normal mother-in-law. She complains about Chi-obaa often. She complains to her friends and to her husband. When Kaneko has coffee with her friends, she tells them, "Okaa-san doesn't help with any of the housework. She doesn't cook, clean or do anything to help me! And her clothes are crazy. She is always wearing bright pink clothes! I feel so embarrassed when I see her. And she is always going out. I never know where she is or what she is doing."

Kenshin and Kaneko have three children. Kazuo is studying business at university in Osaka. Yuka is studying fashion in Kobe, and Mitsuru has just started university in Kyushu. Mitsuru wants to be a teacher.

Kazuo, Yuka and Mitsuru like Chi-obaa very much. When they were young, their mother was always busy doing housework and gardening. Chi-obaa didn't help Kaneko at all. She was always free, so she could play with the children every day. Chi-obaa is interested in everything. She is very modern. Kazuo says his grandmother is more like a friend than an old grandmother.

Chi-obaa fills her time with many hobbies. She takes ukulele classes. She goes to a tai-chi group three days a week. She loves movies, surfing the Internet and listening to music. But especially Chi-obaa likes people. She is always out walking and talking to people in Nakashige-cho. People often tell Chi-obaa their secrets. And sometimes Chi-obaa helps people. She believes that sometimes people need a little push to do the right thing. Chi-obaa is good at pushing.

Now you know a little about Chi-obaa, her friends and family, it's time to read some stories about her.

# CHI-OBAA AND THE GOVERNOR

## 1. MONDAY MORNING

Kenshin Saito works at the prefectural office. He is a quiet man and he works very hard. Every day, he takes a 40 minute train ride from his home in Nakashige-cho to work.

One Monday morning, Kenshin arrived at the office at his usual time. His boss was waiting for him. Tanaka san is a tough boss. Sometimes he is a bully. Kenshin is a little frightened of him.

"Saito. What have you done?" he asked.

"Done?" asked Kenshin. "I'm sorry Tanaka san. I don't understand."

"The Governor wants to see you this morning at 10:00am. I thought it was a mistake. There must be some other person named Saito. But the Governor's secretary says he wants to see Kenshin Saito. And he wants to see you alone. I am very angry and very worried. What have you done?"

"N..n..nothing, Tanaka san. I promise you. I have not done anything wrong." Kenshin was very worried and frightened.

"Go to your desk and think about it," said Tanaka san.

Kenshin went to his desk. He was shaking with fear.

*Did I make some big mistake?* he asked himself. *But if I made some big mistake, Tanaka would know.*

It was now 8:30am. Kenshin had to go to the Governor's office at 10:00am.

*An hour and a half to wait!* thought Kenshin.

Kenshin couldn't concentrate on his work. He went to the toilet many times. He thought about everything he had done. He couldn't think of anything bad.

Finally it was 9:40. Kenshin went to Tanaka san's desk.

"Tanaka san, I will go now," he said.

Tanaka san looked at him. "Whatever trouble you are in, do not make trouble for me or this department. Your co-workers are good people. You are the one who makes trouble."

At 9:50, Kenshin was standing outside the Governor's rooms. The offices were on the third floor. Kenshin had never been there. He knocked very quietly on the secretary's door.

"Come in," said the secretary.

"I..I..I am Kenshin Saito. I don't understand, but my boss says that the Governor wants to see me."

"That is true," said the secretary.

Kenshin knew it was not a good idea. But he could not stop himself.

"Please tell me what I have done wrong," he said to the secretary.

The Governor's secretary is a nice woman. She felt sorry for Kenshin. He looked so frightened. But she couldn't help him.

"I don't know why the Governor wants to see you," she said.

Kenshin waited in the secretary's office. At 10:00 exactly, the secretary telephoned the Governor. "Kenshin Saito is here."

The door of the Governor's office opened. The Governor came out.

"Tea," he said to his secretary. He waved at Kenshin to come into his office.

The Governor's office was very big and it had a beautiful view of the ocean. The desk was huge and empty. In one corner of the room were armchairs and a sofa. The Governor sat in an armchair.

"Please sit," he said to Kenshin pointing to the sofa. Kenshin sat down.

The secretary knocked on the door and carried the tea into the office. She put a cup in front of the Governor. She put a cup in front of Kenshin. She put down the teapot.

"Go," said the Governor. "No phone calls, no visitors."

The secretary and Kenshin were very puzzled. The Governor was behaving in a very strange way.

The secretary went out. She closed the door.

The Governor poured tea.

He looked at Kenshin. "You will say nothing about this meeting. You will not repeat anything to anyone."

Kenshin wondered how he could do this. All his co-workers and Tanaka san, his boss, would ask him about this meeting. He would have to say something. He thought that the Governor did not understand office life.

"Of course not, Your Excellency. I promise you," answered Kenshin.

The Governor was silent for a few moments.

"I believe you have a mother," he said.

"Y..yes, Excellency," answered Kenshin.

"She is sometimes called Chi-obaa?"

"Her name is Mameko Saito but yes, many people c..c...call..." Kenshin was very nervous.

"You are Chi-obaa's son?"

"Y..yes, Excellency. If she has caused some trouble I must ... full responsibility..." The Governor put his hand up and Kenshin stopped talking.

"I have heard about your mother. She sometimes helps people. Solves problems," said the Governor. He was staring at Kenshin.

Kenshin was very worried. He loved Chi-obaa but... *What has my crazy mother done?* he thought. *Has she helped the Governor's enemies?*

"Yes, but...", answered Kenshin.

"Is your mother a gossip?" asked the Governor.

"Oh, no, no. She is a woman with many secrets. Some of them are very old secrets now."

"I want to talk to her," said the Governor. "I have a small private problem. I will visit her this afternoon at 3:00pm. You can go now."

Kenshin got up. He bowed and left the office.

Kenshin went back to his office and sat down at his desk. He opened a file and started working.

"What was it about?" Tanaka san was standing in front of him. "Tell me!"

"Nothing special," answered Kenshin.

Tanaka's face was red. He put his hands on Kenshin's desk. He put his face very close to Kenshin's face. "Tell me!" Tanaka san sounded like an angry cat.

"He wanted to check some facts," said Kenshin.

"If the Governor wanted facts, he could have asked me," Tanaka san was very angry now.

"Maybe he thought I would know the answers better than you, Tanaka san," answered Kenshin. "It is confidential. I was told not to speak about it."

Tanaka san went away. Kenshin felt happy. Maybe Tanaka san would not bully him now.

At 11:00, there was a meeting. The newest office lady served tea.

"The Governor's tea cups are much nicer than ours," said Kenshin. There was silence. Then Matsuura san, who is Tanaka san's favourite said, "You had tea with the Governor?"

Kenshin didn't answer.

## 2. MONDAY AFTERNOON

At lunchtime, Kenshin took his lunchbox outside. He called his wife, Kaneko.

"Kaneko. You must find Chi-obaa. She must be at our house at 3:00pm. The Governor is coming to see her."

Kaneko was amazed. "Why?"

"I don't know. But it is very secret and very private. Please find her. I have to go now. I didn't do any work this morning. Promise me you will not say anything to anyone."

Kaneko felt sorry. She would like to call all her friends. But Kaneko promised she would say nothing.

Kaneko thinks her mother-in-law is very strange. She would like a different mother-in-law. Kaneko is often angry with Chi-obaa. Kaneko is very proud of Kenshin. He has a good job in the prefectural office. But most people in Nakashige-cho call him Chi-obaa's son.

But on this day Kaneko was excited. *Where is okaa-san?* she thought.

Kaneko always wants to know where Chi-obaa is going, and what she is doing, but Chi-obaa doesn't tell her. But Kaneko is like a detective. She watches and sometimes she follows Chi-obaa. She knows a lot about Chi-obaa's schedule. And the Monday schedule is easy to work out.

*It's Monday,* she thought. *Chi-obaa always comes home for lunch at 1:00 on Mondays. She will be here soon.*

The best room was already very clean. Kaneko is a good

housekeeper. But Kaneko cleaned it again. She changed the flowers in the tokonoma alcove. She swept the path to the front door. By 1:00pm she was very tired. Chi-obaa came back. Kaneko put lunch on the table for her.

"Okaa-san," she said. "Kenshin called. It's a secret, but the Governor is coming to see you this afternoon at 3:00. You must be here to meet him."

Chi-obaa stopped eating. "It's not convenient. If he wants to see me, he can call and ask me what time is convenient."

"But it's the Governor," said Kaneko. "Governors are not like other people."

"Well they should be," said Chi-obaa. "I have reading for children at the library this afternoon. I can't be here to meet the Governor."

Kaneko wanted to cry. She sat down at the table. "Please, okaa-san. It might make trouble for Kenshin."

Chi-obaa looked at Kaneko. She thought her daughter-in-law was boring. But Kaneko looked very unhappy. Chi-obaa felt sorry for her. Also Kaneko was right. Maybe the Governor could make trouble for Kenshin.

"I will call Yamamoto san. I will ask her to go to the library to read to the children. I will be here to meet this rude man."

At 3:00, a very expensive car stopped outside the house. The Governor was driving himself.

*Why doesn't he have a driver?* wondered Kaneko. She was hiding behind the curtains and looking outside.

The doorbell rang. Kaneko ran to the door. She knew it was the Governor but she couldn't say so.

"Yes?" she said.

"I want to talk to the woman called Chi-obaa," said the Governor.

"Ah, that would be my mother-in-law, Mameko Saito. "I am the wife of Kenshin Saito. Please come in."

Kaneko showed the Governor to the best room. Chi-obaa was sitting in a large armchair. The Governor looked at Chi-obaa.

Kaneko was standing outside the door.

"Thank you," said the Governor. He shut the door. Kaneko wanted to listen, but she was too frightened. She went out into the garden and took a photograph of the Governor's car with her mobile phone. Then she went back into the house and sat in the kitchen.

She prepared a tea tray in case okaa-san asked for tea.

What did the Governor want to talk to okaa-san about? Would okaa-san be polite? Sometimes okaa-san was very rude to people.

In the best room, the Governor was sitting in an armchair opposite Chi-obaa.

"I want you to help me," he said. "This is a very private family problem."

Chi-obaa said nothing.

"I have a son. He is my only son. He is twenty-three years old. He is at university in Osaka. He has a girlfriend who he wants to marry. But I think he is too young."

"Your wife should talk to him," said Chi-obaa.

"My wife! My wife watches too much television and likes American movies. She is a romantic. She thinks it is lovely."

"My son says he will marry her. I cannot stop him. I am worried. I don't think she is the right person to marry my son," said the Governor.

"There are detective agencies you can use to check on people," said Chi-obaa.

"Of course. I did that. I have to be very careful about my family name. I also have to be careful about what people say and what people know. I found a very good agency. The agency checked on this young woman."

"And…?" asked Chi-obaa.

"They found nothing. Nothing at all," answered the Governor.

"So there is no bad information about her family. She is a good person for your son," said Chi-obaa.

"No! I said nothing. I mean nothing. No family register. No history! Nothing. All they could tell me is that she seems to be a very quiet girl. Even though she works in a bar, she doesn't seem to go out with men, other than my son. But they couldn't find anything about her family. That is why I want you to help. I can't have private detectives making more enquiries. People know she is dating my son and they will talk."

Chi-obaa said nothing.

"I will pay you of course."

Chi-obaa didn't answer.

"It is very important. I want to do good things for the people in this prefecture. If there is some scandal, I will not be elected again."

Chi-obaa said nothing.

"I am proud of my family name. I don't want any scandal. I have other children. Daughters. If my son has a bad marriage it will not be good for them."

Chi-obaa said nothing.

The Governor looked at Chi-obaa. She was very small and she looked very old. But her eyes reminded him of his grandmother. He thought, *This old woman is like my grandmother. She is very strong and very tough. But she will not help me.*

The Governor looked at the floor.

"Please help me. My son is young and sometimes he is silly. But I love him. If this young woman is a good person, I will agree to the marriage. But I must know. I don't want my son to be unhappy."

He looked up at Chi-obaa. For the first time she smiled at him.

"OK. I will try. But if there is no bad history, you must say 'Yes' to the marriage. Though I think they should wait a while."

The Governor was very pleased. "Thank you. Now, how much shall I pay you?"

Chi-obaa looked surprised. "You do not have to pay me! I stopped working for money fourteen years ago. I am retired," she said. "But maybe I will go to Osaka. There will be some costs. You can pay for my costs."

The Governor took out his wallet and gave Chi-obaa some money. "If it's not enough, I will give you more," he promised.

Chi-obaa took her Sailor Moon notebook from the side table and a pink pencil. "Now please tell me everything you know."

"Well, her name is Mimiko Adachi," the Governor began.

When the Governor left, Kaneko ran to the door to farewell him. "You have a nice garden," he said.

Kaneko bowed. The Governor walked to his car, got in and drove away.

Chi-obaa was still sitting in the armchair.

"What did he say?" asked Kaneko.

"You are right. Governors are not like other people. In the beginning I didn't like him. But maybe he is OK. I think I will give him a chance."

Kaneko asked many questions but Chi-obaa wouldn't answer. Kaneko went to look at the picture of the Governor's car. She went to look at her garden. The Governor had said it was very nice!

## 3. MONDAY NIGHT

Kenshin came home from work at the normal time. It had been a strange day at work. Tanaka san was very angry, but Kenshin knew that Tanaka san was a little worried too. If Kenshin had a special relationship with the Governor, he could say things about Tanaka san. Tanaka san did not dare bully Kenshin. So Tanaka san shouted at everyone else but he did not shout at Kenshin.

Kenshin walked into the house at 8:00pm. As usual, the bath was ready. He took a bath and went to the living room. Kaneko had a meal waiting for him. Often he ate alone, but this night Kaneko knelt facing him across the table.

"Where is my mother?"

"She is in her room. She won't talk to anyone. She says she is busy. She says she is going away tomorrow."

"Where? Who with?"

"She didn't say," answered Kaneko.

"What happened today?" asked Kenshin.

"Your mother was difficult. I had trouble persuading her to meet him, but she did. The Governor said my garden was very nice."

"Yes, yes!" Kenshin was impatient. "Tell me everything!"

Kaneko told Kenshin how the governor had a beautiful car, how he had driven himself, that okaa-san didn't offer him tea….

"But why did he come?"

"I don't know," said Kaneko. "Okaa-san wouldn't tell me. But she said she was going away."

In her room Chi-obaa was sending a message to her grandson

Kazuo. Kazuo is a university student in Osaka. Chi-obaa's message was to say that she would be arriving tomorrow and staying a few days.

Kazuo sent back a message to say he was very pleased and looked forward to having his grandmother to stay.

Everyone in the family knows that it is much better to agree to anything that Chi-obaa wants. Also Kazuo is very fond of his grandmother.

Around 10:30pm that night, there was a knock at the door.

"Who can be calling so late at night?" Kaneko asked as she went to answer the door.

It was Chi-obaa's friend Hatsuko Nakamura .

She handed a large supermarket bag to Kaneko.

"Please tell Chi-obaa I did my best but it was very difficult. She is so small."

"What's this?" asked Kaneko.

Hatsuko didn't answer. Like Kazuo, Hatsuko always does what Chi-obaa asks. But she never tells anyone about it. All Chi-obaa's friends know that she likes to have secrets.

## 4. TUESDAY

Early on Tuesday morning, Chi-obaa asked Kaneko to drive her to the bus station.

"Where are you going," asked Kaneko.

"Osaka," said Chi-obaa.

"Osaka? Will you see Kazuo? You could take some food for him. My pickles are very good this year. Kazuo likes my pickles a lot."

"Maybe I will see Kazuo. But I am not taking pickles. I will be busy,"

"What are you going to do?" asked Kaneko.

"Business," said Chi-obaa. "Now please take me to the bus station. I don't want to be late."

Kaneko took Chi-obaa to the highway bus station. Kaneko doesn't like her mother-in-law very much, but she is a kind woman. She felt worried about Chi-obaa. Her mother-in-law looked so small when she climbed onto the bus. Kaneko waited to wave until the bus drove away. Chi-obaa is so small that her head didn't come up to the window. Kaneko couldn't see her, but she stayed and waved goodbye anyway.

The bus arrived in Osaka at lunchtime. Chi-obaa took the subway to Kazuo's apartment. He was at university but he had left a key for Chi-obaa, hidden under a stone by his door.

About an hour later, an old woman came out of Kazuo's apartment building. She was wearing a black dress and old shoes. She had a brown hat, which seemed too big for her. Anyone from Nakashige-cho would recognize the hat. It is Hatsuko Nakamura's favourite. She wears it everywhere. They would not have recognized Chi-obaa. Chi-obaa usually walks quickly. She looks around and is always smiling. This old woman walked slowly and kept her head down. She was carrying two department store bags. One seemed to be filled with a blanket. No one would have believed that under the blanket were an ipod and a mobile phone. The old woman looked very poor.

Chi-obaa walked to an area of Osaka where there were many bars. It took her a long time. The Governor had told her that his son's girlfriend worked in a bar in the Doyama district. Chi-obaa found the bar. She stood on the other side of the road and watched the entrance. It was a quiet time of day. It was open but there were no customers. Chi-obaa knew it would be busy when the offices closed and people finished work. Next to the bar was a game centre and bowling alley. The Governor said that his detectives had told him that the game centre and bowling alley were popular with students. The Governor thought that was how his son had met the girl. He had been at the game centre and then had gone to the bar with his friends to drink.

Chi-obaa knew she would have to wait and watch for a long time. She looked around for somewhere to sit. She was standing in front of a barbershop. Next to the barbershop was a small car park with a row of garbage containers along one side. Someone had left some cardboard piled against the wall. Chi-obaa collected the cardboard and put it on the ground at the front of the car park. Then she took some newspapers from one of her carrier bags. She put the newspapers on top of the cardboard and sat down. She wrapped the blanket around her shoulders. Anyone passing would think she was a homeless person.

She took the photograph the detectives had given the Governor out of her bag. It showed the Governor's son's girlfriend. She looked very young, and was very pretty. Chi-baa sat and watched the bar. At 6:00pm she saw a car stop outside the bar. A young woman kissed the driver and got out of the car. It was the girl in the photograph. Chi-obaa guessed the driver was the Governor's son. Chi-obaa watched everyone who came and went from the bar.

By 7:30 it was getting cold and Chi-obaa was tired. But she didn't have enough information. She called Kazuo. She said, "Please go to the Shangri-la Bar." She gave him the address. "Call me and tell me how many people work there and what they do. Watch the young woman who works there. I think there is only one. I am going back to your apartment."

Chi-obaa packed up her blanket and newspapers and walked slowly down the street. She found a subway station and took the subway back to Kazuo's apartment.

She made herself some tea and ate some cold rice, which was all she could find in Kazuo's refrigerator. Then she lay down on his bed and went to sleep.

The sound of her phone ringing woke her up. She looked at the phone display. It was 11:00pm. It was Kazuo. He was calling from the Shangri-la Bar.

"There are only four people working here. The owner cooks, and his wife takes care of the money. There is an older woman who chops vegetables and washes dishes. Then there is the young girl. She takes orders and delivers food. She is very cute. She talks to everyone, but especially to older businessmen. She is very nice to them!"

"But that's her job," said Chi-obaa. "Bar hostesses always have to entertain the customers."

"No, Chi-obaa. Not in this place. I know it's a bar, but it's more like a family restaurant. The food is very good and there is not much drinking that I could see. Anyway I had to spend most of my money for the week to stay here eating and drinking for three hours."

"That's OK," said Chi-obaa. "I can give you some money. You can come back now. Be sure to stop and buy some food on the way home. I couldn't find anything to eat! I will not be here when you get back. I will come back later."

Chi-obaa hurried. She changed her clothes again. This time she wore normal clothes for an older woman. She looked very clean and respectable. She went down to the street and took a taxi back to Doyama. She stood outside the bar until it closed. She saw a car pull up. The young woman ran out of the bar and jumped into the car. It was a different car than the one she had arrived in. Chi-obaa could see the driver. He was much older, maybe in his fifties. Then a woman came out, she had a carrier bag with an apron inside it. Chi-obaa guessed this was the kitchen helper. She followed her down the road. The woman went to the subway station. Chi-obaa followed her. She followed her onto the platform and got onto the same train carriage. The woman sat in the only empty seat. Chi-obaa waited.

Two stops later, the man sitting next to the kitchen helper got off. Chi-obaa sat down next to the woman. "I want to talk to you," she said.

## 5. WEDNESDAY

    Kindaichi, the owner of the Shangri-la restaurant was surprised on Wednesday afternoon. Mrs Okamoto, his kitchen helper, usually arrived about 3:30 to help chop vegetables before the evening rush. But today, a strange woman arrived. She explained that Mrs Okamoto had a terrible toothache. "It came on suddenly," she said. "She can't even talk. Her mouth is swollen. I am Mrs Okamoto's sister-in-law. She asked me to come. She has written you a letter."
    The letter said that Mrs Okamoto was very sorry. She was in terrible pain so she couldn't work. But she was worried, because Wednesday was quite busy at the Shangri-la. She was sending her sister-in-law, Mrs Saito, who was a very good worker and very honest.
    Kindaichi looked at Mrs Saito. He wondered how she could be Mrs Okamoto's sister-in-law. She looked about thirty years older than Mrs Okamoto.
    "I'm not sure," he said. "The work is hard. Are you strong enough?"
    Mrs Saito stared at him. "I worked in a hotel for twenty years. I know more about hard work than you do!"
    Kindaichi shrugged. "OK. I don't have anyone else and I guess this is only for one night."
    "Thank you," said Mrs Saito. "It might be for one night or for two. Who can say? Now show me the vegetables and I will start."
    Chi-obaa had not peeled vegetables for almost fifteen years. She had retired from cooking at sixty-five, but she hadn't forgotten how to do it. As she peeled and chopped the vegetables, she listened to

the conversation around her.

Kindaichi's wife complained a lot. Especially she complained about Mimiko, the young woman who worked in the bar.

"I don't like her!" she said to her husband. "I want you to tell her to go. She is always making eyes at the older, richer men. She only comes when she feels like it. Think how often she doesn't come to work. Then I have to take money and wait on tables."

Kindaichi seemed to be a kind man.

"But she's a student. She can't work fulltime. She has homework and tests to do. But she needs the money. Imagine! No family and she has to work to pay for her university fees. I know she seems to be very nice to older men, but I think that is because she has no father. I am sure they remind her of her father."

"You are an idiot!" said his wife.

Chi-obaa smiled to herself. Her plan was a very good one! She was finding out many useful things. It had taken a long time to persuade Mrs Okamoto to write the letter and to stay at home. It had taken a lot of the Governor's money too. Chi-obaa had told Mrs Okamoto that her grandson was in love with Mimiko. Chi-obaa said that there was only her grandson and her left. Everyone else in the family had died. When Mrs Okamoto heard that Chi-obaa wanted to check up on Mimiko, she said she was so happy that she would write the letter for free. But she still took the Governor's money.

"That Mimiko's a liar," said Mrs Okamoto. "She says she's a student and that's why she only works part-time. But I know she has another job. She works at a place in Tobita as well. It's called Lolita. She wears a school uniform, so you can guess what kind of place it is. I don't think her name is Mimiko either."

At 6:00, Mimiko came running in.

"Oh, thank goodness I'm not late!" she said. "I had a class and the teacher kept us after the class to talk about exams."

Chi-obaa stared at her. It was the first time she had seen her up close. She was a very pretty girl. Her voice was soft and she wore almost no make-up.

Mimiko saw Chi-obaa staring at her and stared back. Suddenly Chi-obaa saw another person in Mimiko's eyes. A much older person. A dishonest person. The look was only there for a second and then Mimiko lowered her eyes and asked in her soft voice, "Where is Mrs Okamoto?"

Kindaichi explained. Chi-obaa bowed and Mimiko bowed back very politely. Chi-obaa went back to her vegetables and Mimiko went out to the back of the bar to take off her coat.

Chi-obaa had finished the vegetables, so she asked Kindaichi what she should do next. "Take a rest," he said. You'll be very busy washing dishes once the customers arrive."

Chi-obaa went to the back of the restaurant. There was a storeroom and a toilet and a door to the outside.

She didn't see Mimiko, but the door to the toilet was locked. Chi-obaa guessed Mimiko was inside. She went outside and stood under the toilet window. Mimiko was talking on her telephone. She couldn't hear what she was saying but the voice she could hear was like a stranger's voice. Mimiko was speaking in a strong Osaka accent. The voice sounded stronger, harder and older than the little girl voice Mimiko used in the restaurant.

Chi-obaa waited until she heard Mimiko leave the toilet. Then she called Kazuo.

"Are you at home?" she asked.

"Yes, I just got here. When will you come back?" answered Kazuo.

"Sometime," answered Chi-obaa. "I want you to get to this restaurant by 11:00pm. Come on your motor bike. Wait outside. When the girl leaves, someone will come in a car to get her. Follow them. I want to know where she goes. Be careful. It is possible they are not nice people. I will meet you back at your apartment."

# 6. THURSDAY

Chi-obaa left the Shangri-la restaurant at midnight. It had been closed for an hour but there was cleaning to do. She walked to the subway station and took a train back to Kazuo's apartment.

Kazuo did not return until almost 3:00am. Chi-obaa had slept a little but she was worried about Kazuo. Usually, Chi-obaa is sure she is right. She is very confident. But this time Chi-obaa was worried. Kazuo is her favourite grandson. She wondered if she had made a terrible mistake. She didn't know anything about these people. They might be dangerous and she had told Kazuo to follow them.

She was very pleased to see Kazuo when finally, he came back.

"What happened?" she asked.

"An older man came to collect Mimiko," answered Kazuo. "I hurried to get my motorbike and I followed them. After a few blocks I realized something strange. I was following the car with Mimiko in it. But a big black car was also following her. I thought there was something dangerous about the situation, so I was very careful not to get too close. The first car drove to an apartment block in a poor part of Osaka. It drove around to a car park behind the building. I stopped and waited at the corner of the street. The second car, stopped in front of the building. Two men got out. They went into the building and looked at the mail boxes, then they got back in their car and drove away.

"I rode my motor bike around to the back of the building. I was lucky. Someone had parked a car in the man's parking space. I could see and hear him clearly. He had got out of his car and was shouting.

Then Mimiko spoke. She was asking the man to be quiet. She said 'Papa, please be quiet. It doesn't matter. Please don't make a noise. We are supposed to be hiding. This is not a good way to hide!'"

"Hmm," said Chi-obaa. "You did a good job. I think I understand. I know what I must do. Do you have classes today?"

"Not this morning," said Kazuo. "I have a class at 2:30pm. That is good because I am very tired and I need to sleep."

"Can you find the apartment building where you saw Mimiko and her father?" asked Chi-obaa.

"Yes," said Kazuo. "But please Chi-obaa, not now!"

"No, no. We need to sleep. And she will be in bed by now. We will leave here at lunchtime. You will take me to the place. You will show me the car park. You will leave me there. Then, you can go to university."

When they left Kazuo's apartment, Chi-obaa was wearing her favourite tracksuit and Kazuo's spare motor bike helmet. She climbed onto the back of Kazuo's motor bike. He took her to the car park behind the apartment building. He showed her the parking space where the man had tried to park his car. Then Chi-obaa gave him back his helmet and he rode away.

Chi-obaa looked at the number on the parking space. As she had thought, it was easy to work out which apartment the parking space belonged to. The parking space was labelled 7-11. So the apartment number was 7-11. She went into the building and took the elevator to the 7th floor. She rang the bell of apartment 11. She heard someone come to the door but the door didn't open. She thought there was someone looking through the spyhole. She called out.

"I am Mameko Saito. You met me at the restaurant last night. I found something that belongs to you."

The door opened. Mimiko was standing in the doorway.

"What is it?" asked Mimiko. "What did you find that belongs to me?"

"Nothing," said Chi-obaa. "But I have some information that will be very useful to you. I know that you and your father are in danger. I think you should talk to me."

Mimiko stood back and Chi-obaa walked into the apartment.

"Go in there," said Mimiko pointing to a living room. "I will bring some tea." Chi-obaa noticed that she was using the adult voice not the little girl voice.

Chi-obaa went into the living room and sat in a chair next to the dining table.

Mimiko brought the tea and handed a cup to Chi-obaa. She sat down and stared at her.

"I don't know who you are. I don't know what you know. I have nothing to say to you. But I want to know how you found me here."

Chi-obaa stared back. "You don't have to say anything. I want you to listen to me. Then I will tell you what you should do."

Mimiko laughed. "You! You are a silly old woman. I think you should go now."

Chi-obaa didn't move. "Listen. I will tell you a story. There was a father and a daughter. Maybe there were more people in the family, I don't know.

"The father got into trouble. I think he owes money. Perhaps he owes money to gangsters. Gangsters are very good at finding people. The father and the daughter have been hiding from the gangsters for a long time. The daughter can't go to university or find a good job. She needs a job where the pay is cash and no one worries about IDs or tax or health insurance. She uses many different names. She has worked at many different places. When people get too interested or friendly, she finds another job. She works at places like Lolita in Tobita. She wears school uniforms with very short skirts or dresses like a maid or a nurse. These are not nice places to work but the money is good. But the daughter wants more. She hopes to find a man to marry her. The men at places like Lolita have no romantic ideas about the women that work there. Their interest is sex not marriage. So the daughter creates another identity. She gets a second job at a small respectable bar and restaurant. She says her name is Mimiko. She tells the people at this restaurant that she is twenty-two years old. Mimiko is very shy and sweet. She says she has no family. She says she is a student. This is the kind of place where maybe she can meet a rich husband. Then she meets a university student. He is from a rich and powerful family. He falls in love with Mimiko. He wants to marry her. But she doesn't plan to marry him. She has another idea."

Mimiko was staring at Chi-obaa. "Are you a witch?" she shouted.

"Oh. My story is correct then?"

Mimiko didn't answer.

"The university student is from a rich and powerful family. But the daughter doesn't want to marry him. He is too young. He is maybe six or seven years younger. He is not a man. He has no money of his own. But maybe the boy's father will pay a lot of money to stop the marriage. This is a much better idea."

Mimiko was very angry but Chi-obaa could see that she was also very frightened. "You don't know that this story is true. You are only guessing."

Chi-obaa bowed her head. "That is true. I am only guessing. But I know many people. If I tell them this story, they will believe me. You will have to hide from the gangsters but you will also have to hide from some very powerful people. These powerful people have a lot of influence with the police. You will have two enemies. I think your life is very difficult now. I can make your life much more difficult."

Mimiko could not believe what was happening. This tiny little old lady in a pink track suit was a devil.

"I can't tell you anything. It's too dangerous. Please don't ask me," said Mimiko.

"I don't want you to tell me anything. I am not interested in your father. I am not interested in your real name. I don't want to know your history. I want you to do something. I want you to call the university student. I want you to invent a story. A university scholarship to France, a sick aunt in Okinawa - anything. I am sure you are very good at stories. Break up with him. Do it nicely. Try not to hurt him. Then disappear. Kill Mimiko. Make another identity. That's all."

"Why should I do that?" asked Mimiko. "What will you do for me?"

"I will never tell anyone what I know. I won't do anything to help you, but I won't do anything to make your life more difficult."

Mimiko sighed. "I am frightened of my father's enemies, but I think I am more frightened of you. I will do what I you ask."

"Good." Chi-obaa stood up to go. "Do it, and do it well. If you don't, I will find you."

She walked to the door of the apartment. As she walked out the door, she turned. "One thing."

"Yes?" asked Mimiko.

"Last night when your father collected you from the Shangri-la restaurant, you were followed. There were two men. These men had nothing to do with me. So I guess they are your father's enemies.

They know you and your father are living here. I think you are in danger. You should leave here immediately."

Chi-obaa went away. She went back to Kazuo's apartment. She packed her clothes and left a note for Kazuo. She also left him the rest of the Governor's money. She put the apartment key under the stone and took a taxi to the bus station. When she was in the bus, on her way back to Nakashige-cho, she called the Governor.

"What did you find out?" he asked.

"That is not important," said Chi-obaa. "You wanted to rescue your son from a bad situation. I am calling to tell you that he will never marry the girl from the bar. His heart may be broken a little, but he is safe."

"But who was she?" asked the Governor. "What was wrong with her?"

"I don't think you need to know that," said Chi-obaa. She was strong. "I have done what you asked. Please remember that one day, I might ask you to do something for me."

Chi-obaa turned her telephone off. She closed her eyes. It had been a very tiring week.

# CHI-OBAA AND THE TRICYCLE

## 1. A PRESENT FOR HATSUKO

One morning, about five years ago, Taihei Nakamura was eating breakfast with his wife, Noriko. Taihei Nakamura owns the hair salon in Nakashige-cho.

"I'm going to buy my mother a tricycle," he said.

Noriko stopped eating and looked at him.

"A what?" she asked.

"A tricycle. It's like a bicycle, but with three wheels. Two at the back and one at the front."

"Why?" asked Noriko.

"My mother is almost seventy-five years old. She still rides a bicycle. It is too dangerous," said Taihei.

"Why don't you tell her to stop?" asked Noriko.

"I tried," said Taihei. "But she doesn't listen to me. She says she has ridden a bicycle for more than sixty years. She likes it. She says it is too far to walk to the supermarket. So I think a tricycle would be a good idea."

"But tricycles are for very small children," said Noriko.

"It is possible to buy tricycles for adults," said Taihei. "It will be much safer if my mother has a tricycle."

Noriko stood up. "Do what you think is best. I agree. It is dangerous if your mother rides a bicycle. It's time to open the salon. Please hurry."

Taihei Nakamura is a good son. He looks after his mother very well. But the reason for buying his mother a tricycle was because he also cares about the people in Nakashige-cho. The truth was that his mother on a bicycle was very dangerous for other people.

Hatsuko Nakamura is very popular in Nakashige-cho. She has lived all her life in the town. She is a very kind women and people like her very much. But people always said "I wish Nakamura san would not ride a bicycle. Someday, she will kill someone."

Hatsuko had never learned to ride a bicycle in a straight line. Sometimes she cycled in the middle of the road. Sometimes she went suddenly to the left or the right. Hatsuko didn't notice cars, traffic lights, other bicycles, or other people when she was riding. The roads in Nakashige-cho are very narrow. When people saw Hatsuko coming along the road on her bicycle, they would pick up their children, hide behind lamp posts, or go into the nearest shop. Taihei Nakamura was right. His mother was very kind and responsible most of the time. But when she was on a bicycle, she was very dangerous.

Taihei ordered the tricycle. He gave it to his mother. It was the same size as a normal bicycle but there were two wheels at the back. Hatsuko was pleased.

"It has a big basket between the two back wheels. That will be very useful," she said.

Taihei is a very good hairdresser, but maybe he is not too smart about other things. The tricycle has some good points. His mother doesn't ride all over the road. She can ride in a straight line. But the tricycle is wider than a bicycle, and the streets of Nakashige-cho are narrow. Now Hatsuko rides in a straight line down the middle of the street. When she wants to stop, she leaves her tricycle in the middle of the street. Cars often have to wait until Hatsuko has finished her shopping. And Hatsuko likes to chat with the shopkeepers and other customers. Life in Nakashige-cho is not so dangerous now that Hatsuko has a tricycle. But life is much more inconvenient instead.

Now people say, "I wish Nakamura san would not ride a tricycle. Someday, a driver will kill her."

Hatsuko keeps her tricycle in the car park next to the hairdressing salon. She never locks her tricycle.

"I have the only tricycle in Nakashige," she says. "No one will steal it. If anyone stole my tricycle, everyone would know it was mine."

One morning, Hatsuko went out of her apartment, down the stairs, and into the car park. She was going to the supermarket to shop for herself and for Noriko. But her tricycle wasn't there!

Hatsuko was shocked! She sat on the seat outside the hair salon. *Where is my tricycle?* she asked herself.

Just then, Hatsuko saw Chi-obaa walking along the street. Chi-obaa was pushing her shopping walker. Chi-obaa likes her shopping walker very much. It has four wheels, a brake, and a seat. The seat is very useful for long conversations when she meets a friend.

"Chi-obaa! Chi-obaa!" shouted Hatsuko. "Come here! I have a problem."

Chi-obaa came to Hatsuko. She put the brake on her shopping walker and sat on the seat.

"What's the problem?" asked Chi-obaa.

"My tricycle is not there. It has gone!" answered Hatsuko.

Chi-obaa was surprised. "Who would take your tricycle?"

"I don't know," said Hatsuko.

"When was the last time you rode it?" asked Chi-obaa.

"Three days ago. But it was there yesterday. I saw it. I saw it at about 7:30pm, and now it is gone! And I must go to the supermarket. I told Noriko I would go shopping for her. It's going to be a busy day in the hair salon today."

Chi-obaa stood up. "Here. Take my shopping walker to the supermarket. The box under the seat is not as big as your basket, but maybe it will be OK."

"Thank you," said Hatsuko. "It's OK to walk to the supermarket, but I don't like carrying shopping back home. What are you going to do?"

Chi-obaa sat on the seat outside the hair salon. "I am going to think," she answered.

## 2. WHAT DID YOU SEE AND HEAR?

Chi-obaa sat outside the hair salon. She knew that people got angry with Hatsuko because she rode her tricycle in the middle of the street. Car drivers often had to wait a long time. But she didn't think anyone would steal Hatsuko's tricycle.

Chi-obaa looked up and down the street. She looked at the car park. The bicycle disappeared after 7:30 last night, and before 10:00 this morning. Someone must have seen or heard something, she thought.

Chi-obaa took out her mobile phone and called Hanae.

"Hanae," said Chi-obaa. "Hatsuko's bicycle has disappeared. I need your help."

"Now?" asked Hanae. "I was planning to go to the manicurist."

"Now, please. We must find Hatsuko's tricycle," answered Chi-obaa.

"Many people in this town will be very happy if they hear Hatsuko has lost her tricycle," said Hanae.

"I know. But please meet me at the hair salon as soon as you can," said Chi-obaa.

"OK," said Hanae. "I will be there in ten minutes."

Chi-obaa took out her Sailor Moon notebook and a pencil. She wrote down a list of names.

When Hanae arrived, Chi-obaa showed her the notebook.

"These are all the people who live near here, and who might have been on this street between 7:30 last night and 10:00 this morning. Can you think of anyone else?"

Hanae read the list. She took the pencil from Chi-obaa and added a few more names.

"I think that's everyone we know," she said. "But none of these people would ever steal Hatsuko's tricycle."

"Maybe not," said Chi-obaa. "But someone might have seen or heard something."

Hanae and Chi-obaa divided the list. Hanae lived between the shopping street and the railway station. She could talk to all the people who walked to the station in the morning and walked back home at night. Some people who lived far from the station used bicycles. Every day, they rode to the station in the morning and back at night.

Chi-obaa could talk to everyone living near the hair salon. She could also talk to the junior high school and high school students. They were often late coming home from school.

Chi-obaa and Hanae made a plan to meet the next morning in Hanae's apartment. Then Hanae went to catch the train to the city and Chi-obaa went into the hair salon.

"Nakamura san, I am sorry to disturb you. Could I speak to you for a few minutes?" asked Chi-obaa.

"Chi-obaa. I have a client now. Please wait until the salon is closed," answered Taihei.

Taihei was cutting Michiko Sato's hair. She smiled.

"Nakamura san. It's okay. Please talk to Chi-obaa. I can wait."

Taihei and Chi-obaa went outside.

"Your mother's tricycle has disappeared," said Chi-obaa. "We should find it. Did you hear or see anything strange last night or early this morning?"

"What time?" asked Taihei.

"After 7:30 last night. Your mother noticed her tricycle was missing at about 10:00 this morning."

"I left the salon to go home about 7:00 last night," said Taihei. "I came back about 7:45 this morning. I didn't see or hear anything strange."

"OK," said Chi-obaa. "Please ask your wife, your staff and everyone in the salon the same question."

Taihei looked at Chi-obaa. "Chi-obaa," he said. "I don't know where my mother's tricycle is. But maybe it is better if she doesn't find it. People are always complaining to me about it."

This made Chi-obaa angry. "Nakamura san! Your mother is very unhappy. She likes her tricycle! We must find it!"

"Yes, yes. Of course, Chi-obaa. I'm sorry. I will do everything you say."

Chi-obaa had a busy day. She talked to everyone who lived near the salon. No one had seen or heard anything.

Hatsuko came to Chi-obaa's house with the shopping walker.

"Thank you," she said. "It was very useful. But it is not as good as my tricycle."

In the evening, Chi-obaa talked to the junior high school and high school students. She talked to Keita Sato. Keita said he hadn't seen or heard anything, but Chi-obaa thought he knew something.

"Keita. Tell me everything. What do you know?" she asked.

"Chi-obaa. I told you. I rode down the street and past the hair salon at about 8:00pm. I think the tricycle was in the car park. But I'm not sure. I didn't see anything or anyone unusual."

"But Keita. I think you know something. Please tell me."

Keita was not happy. "It is a secret, Chi-obaa. I promised."

"Keita, I am very good at secrets," said Chi-obaa. "You must tell me."

"Well," said Keita. "You know my friend Sho Wada?"

"Sho in the basketball team? The one who lives in that old house out of town?"

"Yes, him. Well, his family has some money troubles. I don't know why. He has a part-time job. It's a big secret. Our school doesn't like us to have part-time jobs during the school year, and the basketball coach would drop him from the team if he knew."

"How can Sho find time to work part-time?" asked Chi-obaa. "He has to go to school and practice basketball."

"I know," said Keita. "That's why his part-time job is at night. It's really bad. He works from 7:30pm. to midnight in a bar. It is opposite the bank near the railway station. He works in the back of the bar, washing glasses and carrying boxes. He hates it. And he is so tired all the time."

"Poor Sho," said Chi-obaa. "I must think about his bad situation."

"Yes," said Keita. "Please try to help him. But you must never say that I told you."

"I won't. But what has this got to do with the missing tricycle?" asked Chi-obaa.

"Maybe nothing. But Sho told me that last night, about 11:00, he was outside carrying boxes. He heard a man leaving the bar and going onto the street. Then there was a loud noise. The noise came from the street. He thought it was a car accident and he went to look. The man from the bar had fallen off a bicycle. The bicycle was on the ground. The man was walking along the middle of the road. Sho thought he was very drunk. But there was something else. There were two men in the walkway, down the side of the bank. They had a ladder. When they saw Sho they took the ladder away. Sho was a little frightened, but he went to look. He couldn't see the men, but saw that the ladder had been next to the cash machine."

"What did he do?" asked Chi-obaa.

"He didn't do anything. He thought the men might come back, so he didn't touch anything. He didn't say anything, because his job must be a secret," said Keita.

"Thank you for telling me that, Keita. I don't know if it means anything. I will try to think of some way to help Sho and his family, and I will keep his secret."

## 3. THE TRICYCLE THIEF

The next morning, Chi-obaa went to Hanae's apartment.

"How is Hatsuko?" asked Hanae.

"I don't know. She's helping in the hair salon today," said Chi-obaa. "What did you find out?"

"Nothing," said Hanae. "I talked to so many people. I am so tired. No one heard or saw anything strange."

"Nothing?" said Chi-obaa.

"Well there's just one thing," said Hanae. "But maybe it means nothing."

"What is it?" asked Chi-obaa.

"You know Tanaka san who works at the railway station?"

"Yes," said Chi-obaa. "His wife left him and took their children. She has gone to live with her parents."

"That's right," said Hanae. "Well, they say that he is drinking a lot now. I usually see him every day. He passes my apartment when I am having breakfast. But I didn't see him yesterday, and I didn't see him this morning. So I went to the railway station. The manager there said he didn't go to work yesterday, and that he was not at work today."

"Does he ride a bicycle to work?" asked Chi-obaa.

"Yes," said Hanae. "He always rides a bicycle."

"Do you know where he lives?" asked Chi-obaa.

"I can find out," answered Hanae.

Hanae called the post office. The manager of the post office is a little in love with Hanae so it was easy to find out where Tanaka san lived. It was too far to walk, so Chi-obaa called her daughter-in-law.

"Kaneko. I am at Yamamoto san's apartment. I want you to come here in the car. I want you to drive us somewhere."

Hanae was amazed. "But Chi-obaa, we could take a taxi. You can't tell your daughter-in-law to drive us. She might be busy."

"She is never busy," said Chi-obaa. "It is good for her to do something."

Kaneko came to Hanae's apartment. She drove Chi-obaa and Hanae to Tanaka san's house. It was a little outside Nakashige-cho on a farm road. Kaneko stopped the car outside the house.

"Thank you," said Chi-obaa getting out of the car. "You can go now. I will call you when we need you to come back."

Hanae got out of the car. She bowed to Kaneko. "Thank you so much. We have disturbed your day. I am so sorry." She bowed again.

Chi-obaa took Hanae's arm. "Come on!" she said. "Stop wasting time."

The house had many trees around it. There was a fence at the front. The gate was open. Chi-obaa and Hanae walked into the garden in front of the house. It was a beautiful traditional garden, but it was very untidy. Hatsuko's tricycle sat in the middle of a stone path. Chi-obaa and Hanae walked towards the house. The front door was open.

Chi-obaa and Hanae stood at the door.

"Excuse me! Hello!" shouted Hanae.

There was no reply. There was no sound.

"I think there is something wrong," said Hanae. "Tanaka san did not go to work."

"Hello!" Hanae shouted again.

There was no reply.

"Come on," said Chi-obaa. "Let's go in."

They found Tanaka san lying on the living room floor. He was still wearing his work uniform. There was blood on the legs of his trousers. He was snoring loudly. There was a sake bottle and a whisky bottle on the floor. It took a long time to wake him up.

"He needs to go to bed," said Hanae. "He came home drunk. Then every time he woke up, he must have drunk some more. He has become ill from drinking too much alcohol."

"Yes," said Chi-obaa. "But I want him to talk to us first."

Hanae once lived in a geisha house. She knows a lot about men who have drunk too much sake.

"Leave it to me," she said.

In a short time, Tanaka san was sitting up and talking. He was very worried because he had not gone to work. He didn't know what day it was.

Hanae told him, "You missed two days of work! You must know that too much sake and whisky is bad for you!"

Tanaka san agreed. He agreed that drinking in bars is bad, because he could not remember very much about the night that Hatsuko's tricycle was stolen.

"I remember leaving work," he said. "I remember going to the bar. Then I don't remember anything until you woke me up."

Hanae looked at him. "It is very dangerous to drink so much that you can't remember. Are you crazy? You will destroy your brain and your body."

"Do you know why Nakamura san's tricycle is in your garden?" asked Chi-obaa.

"No," said Tanaka san. "I have no idea."

"OK," said Chi-obaa. "I think I know. I will tell you."

"Please tell me," said Tanaka san.

"Two nights ago, you went to a bar. You drank a lot. About 11:00pm you left the bar. You were very drunk. You tried to ride your bicycle but you couldn't. You fell on the ground. That is why you have blood on your trousers. You left your bicycle in the road and walked away."

"How do you know this?" asked Tanaka san.

"Someone saw you," answered Chi-obaa.

"Oh, no!" said Tanaka san.

"Don't worry," said Chi-obaa. "The person who saw you will not say anything. You walked a little way, but then you saw Nakamura san's tricycle. You had an idea. You would borrow the tricycle. You would ride it home. The next day, very early, you would take it back."

"Is that what I did?" asked Tanaka san.

"Yes I think so," said Chi-obaa. "But you didn't take it back because you got so drunk and then when you woke up you kept drinking. Now what are we going to do?"

"Tanaka san is sick. He cannot be left alone," said Hanae. "He is poisoned by alcohol. So he needs someone to look after him. But we can't tell anyone. If we tell anyone, he might lose his job at the railway station."

"That would not be good," said Chi-obaa. "He would drink himself to death very soon."

Chi-obaa and Hanae sat on the sofa and thought. Tanaka san started snoring again.

Then Chi-obaa had an idea.

"Hanae. Do you think Tanaka san has any money?"

"What do you mean?"

"Do you think he could pay someone to look after him?"

Hanae took out her mobile phone. She went into the garden and she called the bank. There is only one bank in Nakashige-cho, so everyone uses the same one. She spoke to the manager. Hanae is very good-looking, and very charming. The manager of the post office might be a little in love with Hanae, but the bank manager is very much in love with her. He has asked her to marry him. The bank manager is only 65 years old and Hanae is 78, although she says she is 70. The bank manager says age doesn't matter. Chi-obaa thinks it is because the bank manager knows how much money Hanae has. She is a very rich woman. But Chi-obaa doesn't say so.

Hanae was very nice to the bank manager. After a few minutes she came back.

"He has quite a lot of money," she said. "He has enough money to pay someone to look after him."

"Good," said Chi-obaa. "Now I must find a telephone book." She found the telephone book in the bookcase. She found the telephone number for the Wada family and punched it into her phone. Someone answered.

"Wada san?" asked Chi-obaa. "I am calling for one of your neighbours, Tanaka san. He has fallen ill and he needs someone to look after him."

The telephone conversation took a long time. But when Chi-obaa said goodbye to Wada san, everything was organized. Wada san and her husband would come in their car. They would take Tanaka san back to their house. They would look after him. Tanaka san would pay them when he was better. Chi-obaa promised there would be no problem with the money. They would take him to the hospital immediately if he became worse. They would tell everyone he had influenza. Somehow, without saying anything, Chi-obaa had told Wada san, that if anyone found out what was wrong with Tanaka san, some Wada family secret would be told.

Hanae was listening. She thought it must be very convenient to know so many secrets. Chi-obaa could get people to do things for her. It was so easy.

Then Hanae rang the railway station. She told them that Tanaka san had very severe influenza and had lost his voice. He was staying with neighbours until he recovered. "No," she said to the manager of the railway station. "I don't know the neighbours. I have never met them. I got this information from a friend of mine. I thought you would like to know."

When Hanae hung up, she looked at Chi-obaa. Chi-obaa was laughing at her. "You are a good liar, Hanae!"

Hanae disagreed.

"Not at all! Everything I said was true. I have never met the Wada family and you told me about the plan."

"It's a pity you're too old, Hanae. You would make a great politician!"

"Who says I'm too old? I would like to be a politician."

This interesting conversation was stopped by noises outside. It was Wada san and her husband. They had come to take Tanaka san to their house. Mr Wada is a big man. He wrapped Tanaka san in a blanket. He was strong enough to carry him to the car.

Chi-obaa and Hanae followed with Mrs Wada. Hanae was explaining what Mrs Wada should do to help Tanaka san recover. Mr Wada stopped by Hatsuko's tricycle. "I see you found the tricycle as well. You have been busy today!"

He laughed and went to the car. He put Tanaka san on the back seat. He and his wife climbed in the front, and they drove away.

The old ladies went back into the house, and tidied up a little. They emptied the refrigerator, and threw out all the alcohol they could find. It was not very much. Poor Tanaka san had drunk almost everything.

Then another telephone call.

Chi-obaa told Hatsuko's son, Taihei, that he would find Hatsuko's tricycle in some bushes at the crossroads just outside Nakashige-cho. He said he would go there after the salon was closed. His wife would drive him, and he would ride the tricycle back.

They closed the door to the house and Hanae pushed the tricycle down the hill to the crossroads. They pushed the tricycle off the road, and Hanae called a taxi. Chi-obaa was annoyed about this.

"Kaneko can come and get us," she complained. "Why spend money?"

"Because you are not nice to Kaneko. You can do what you like, but I was embarrassed before. I will not be embarrassed again."

Chi-obaa was quiet while they waited for the taxi. Hanae wondered what was wrong. The problem was that Chi-obaa was sure she had forgotten something. She thought about everything they had done. They had found Hatsuko's tricycle. They had found Tanaka san, discovered his problem, and arranged for his recovery. She had found a way to get some extra money into the Wada family, although maybe not enough for their son Sho to stop working. What had she forgotten?

In the taxi she remembered. "Can I come to your apartment?" she asked Hanae. "I need to go out tonight."

## 4. SHO

Hanae and Chi-obaa ate dinner in Hanae's apartment. It's strange. Everyone knows that Chi-obaa doesn't cook, but no one seems to notice that Hanae doesn't cook either. Chi-obaa sat and watched television while Hanae took a bath. Then Hanae called the restaurant on the ground floor of her apartment block.

Twenty minutes later, the doorbell rang. Hanae took a tray of used dishes to the door and carried back another tray with two three-course meals.

"I didn't know that restaurant did home deliveries," said Chi-obaa curiously.

"They don't," smiled Hanae. "But they only have to get in the elevator to bring me food. They don't mind at all. I keep a monthly account with them."

After dinner, Chi-obaa thanked Hanae and left the apartment. It was only a short walk to the bar opposite the bank. She didn't go into the bar. She walked around to the back of the bar and stood in the parking area behind it. Four cars and a small truck were parked there. The truck was very old, dirty, and smelt of fish. A pile of empty bottles and crates were stacked in one corner. The car park was dark, but there was a little light from an open door. It was the back entrance to the bar.

Chi-obaa waited. After a few minutes a young boy came out of the door. He was carrying a crate of empty sake bottles. He put the crate on the ground.

Chi-obaa called out, "Sho? Sho, is that you?"

Sho looked up. "Yes, but who are you?"

Chi-obaa walked into the light. "You know me."

"Chi-obaa! What are you doing here? You mustn't tell anyone you saw me."

"I won't. But I want to talk to you."

"Why?"

"Two nights ago you saw something at the bank. I want you to tell me about it."

"It wasn't anything. How did you know about that? I only told Keita!"

"Don't be angry with Keita. He is a good friend to you. He is worried about you. It is not good for you to be working here. And two nights ago you saw some people at the bank."

"Keita should keep his mouth shut. It wasn't anything. Just two men with a ladder. They didn't seem to be doing anything wrong. "

"Show me where they were," Chi-obaa ordered.

Sho was angry, but he said "OK!" and walked out to the street with Chi-obaa. They walked across the road and Sho pointed.

"They were over there. One man was up the ladder and the other man had a computer or something. He was down on the ground and talking."

Chi-obaa looked. They had been at the cash machine outside the bank. She looked up. There was a security camera on the wall.

"Was the man doing something with the security camera?" she asked.

"Maybe," said Sho. "I have to go back to work. I can't lose my job."

They walked back across the road.

"Why do you have this job?" asked Chi-obaa.

Sho stopped. "I can't say."

"I am very good at secrets," said Chi-obaa. "But I can't help you if you don't tell me."

"Keita says you are OK, but…" Sho did not seem to be sure about this. "If I tell you, you can never tell anyone."

"Ask Keita," answered Chi-obaa. "He will tell you that I never repeat secrets."

Sho was not sure, but he was very young and his life was too difficult.

"It's my brother," he said. "My older brother. He got a job in

Kobe. He liked it but the pay was very low. He didn't have enough money. So he took money from the company. The boss found out. He said he would not tell the police if my brother paid the money back. My parents are trying to find enough money to pay the company, but it's a lot. It also costs my family a lot of money for me to go to high school. No one in my family has ever gone to high school. I am the first. My parents think I should stop studying, and get a job. But I love it. I want to go to university. My father said I could stay at high school if I paid for it myself. So I got this job. But it is so difficult!"

Chi-obaa looked at Sho.

"I understand. I understand how you feel. But I understand your parents' ideas too. Please be patient. I will find a way to help you."

Just then there was a lot of noise from the bar – shouting and laughing.

"What's happening in there?" asked Chi-obaa.

"It's the fish man," explained Sho. "The man who drives around in his truck and sells fish to housewives. He is very happy tonight. He is buying drinks for everyone."

"Why?" Chi-obaa was surprised. The fish man did not have a lot of money. His truck was very old, and he lived in a tiny old house that was slowly falling down around him.

"His son has sent him money. He will take the money to the city tomorrow and buy a new truck. So, tonight he is celebrating."

Sho smiled and thought, *My life seems hard, but I think the fish man's life has been much harder. I am happy for him. But I hope he doesn't spend too much of his new money buying drinks for other people.*

Chi-obaa was tired. She was sure there was an answer to all of this, but she couldn't think what it was. She said goodnight to Sho, and told him not to worry. Then she walked home.

## 5. THE FISH MAN

At 9:00 the next morning. Chi-obaa was sitting on the seat outside the hair salon. She was watching Hatsuko clean her tricycle.

"Maybe it was OK for someone to steal my bicycle. I have it back now, but why is it so dirty?" Hatsuko complained.

"Hmmm." Chi-obaa wasn't listening. "Who owns that dirty old truck in the car park?"

"That's Hamada san's truck. You know, Hamada san. The fish man."

"I saw it last night, but why is it here?"

"He came early this morning," Hatsuko explained. "Today is a very important day for him. But he drank too much last night. His hands were shaking so much this morning that he couldn't shave. He came here and asked Taihei to give him a shave."

Just then Hamada san came out of the salon. He was smiling.

"Good morning ladies!" he said. "I look smart, don't I? I'm going to get the money from the bank. The bank's not open yet but I am taking the 10:00 train. So I'll get my money from the cash machine. Then I'm going on the train to get my new truck. My son is buying it for me!"

He didn't take his old truck from the car park. He walked down the road towards the bank.

"Silly old man," said Hatsuko. "He is so proud of his son. He doesn't understand that his son is ashamed of him. His son thinks it is easier to send his father the money for a new truck, than to come to Nakashige-cho to visit him."

Hatsuko continued talking. "It is such a big event. He even bought a new bag to carry the cash in. The money to pay for the truck I mean. He's not lucky. With his luck the cash machine will be out of order as well."

Chi-obaa was interested. "Out of order as well as what?"

"You don't know?" Hatsuko was surprised. Chi-obaa usually knew everything.

"The security cameras at the cash machine aren't working. Yesterday? Maybe the day before, they stopped working. The bank manager told Taihei they couldn't be fixed until next week."

Chi-obaa stood up.

"Hatsuko! Hamada san is going to take the money for his new truck from the cash machine?"

"Yes."

"He's going to take the money in cash?"

"Yes. That's why he bought a new bag. It's a lot of money."

"And the bank is closed until 10.00, and the security cameras are not working?"

"That's what I heard."

"Has Hamada san told other people about this?"

"Of course. He's told everyone. He's so proud and happy," Hatsuko explained.

Chi-obaa ran to Hatsuko's tricycle. She sat in the basket at the back.

"Hatsuko! Now! Ride to the bank as quickly as you can!"

Chi-obaa's friends always do what she tells them to do. Hatsuko got onto her tricycle and started riding towards the bank.

The next events were the main news in Nakashige-cho for weeks afterwards. People talked about how Hatsuko rode her tricycle at high speed down the road. Chi-obaa was in the basket at the back. She was shouting to the bank manager on her mobile phone. Then she called the police. The nearest police station is in the next town.

People told each other how the tricycle arrived at the bank. It was a great story. A car was parked outside the bank. A man ran out of the cash machine booth. He was carrying Hamada san's new bag. He jumped into the car, and the driver accelerated down the street towards the railway station. A woman jumped in front of the car. It was Hanae. She threw a bottle at the car. It smashed on the windscreen.

The driver tried to reverse, but there was a tricycle in the middle of the street. The car couldn't go anywhere.

Then the bank manager and his staff ran out of the bank. They were shouting. They surrounded the car and stopped the thieves from getting out.

Next the police arrived. They arrested the thieves. The police found Hamada san lying on the floor of the cash machine booth. He had a big lump on his head where the thieves had hit him.

Nakashige-cho is a very quiet town. Nothing happens there. The event at the bank was a big talking point for days. Very few people were on the street when it happened, but somehow, everyone believed they knew the whole story.

One mystery, at least for Chi-obaa and Hatsuko, was: "Why was Hanae on the street outside the bank with a bottle at 9:10 in the morning?"

Hanae is a good friend of both of them. So they asked her.

Hanae explained. "I thought I should give the bank manager a little present because he had told me about Tanaka san's bank account. I don't like to go to liquor stores to buy alcohol. I don't like to buy it in the supermarket either. People talk about you if you buy alcohol. The owner of the bar opposite the bank is an old friend. When I want to buy some whisky or sake, I go to see him. He sells it to me, and no one knows.

"I was walking across the road to the bank. I had a bottle of whisky. I was going to leave it as a present for the bank manager. I saw the man run out of the cash machine booth. No one runs out of a bank unless they are a robber. I wanted to stop the car, so I threw the bottle at its windscreen."

"You are a heroine!" said Hatsuko.

It has been an exciting week for the people of Nakashige-cho. The police returned the money to Hamada san. He was still in hospital, but his head injury was not so bad. He could buy his new truck as soon as he got out of hospital.

But almost immediately, everyone in Nakashige-cho had something new to talk about.

The owner of a sports shop in Tokyo had decided to give a high school scholarship to a member of the Nakashige-cho high school basketball team. The owner had been born in Nakashige-cho, but had gone to live in the city, and he had made a lot of money. The scholarship was big news. But the most surprising thing was that the scholarship had been given to Sho Wada.

"Why Sho?" people asked. Everyone knew that Keita Sato was the best basketball player in the high school team.

Keita wasn't saying anything. He was very pleased. He didn't know how Chi-obaa had done it.

Keita might be young, but he is quite smart. He knows that Chi-obaa has many secrets, and maybe there are ways of using secrets well. Keita knows he is the best player in the high school team. He also knew that his friend Sho could stay at high school now because he had this scholarship. This was a good result.

# THANK YOU

Thank you for reading Chi-obaa and Her Town. (Word count: 13,773) We hope you enjoyed it. We have two more graded readers with stories from Nakashige-cho:
Chi-obaa and Friends
The Witches of Nakashige

There are quizzes about this book on our free study site I Talk You Talk Press EXTRA. http://italk-youtalk.com

If you would like to read more graded readers, please visit our website
http://www.italkyoutalk.com

Other Level 4 graded readers include
Chi-obaa and Friends
End House (Old Secrets – Modern Mysteries Book 2)
On the Run (Old Secrets – Modern Mysteries Book 3)
The Blue Lace Curtain (Old Secrets – Modern Mysteries Book 1)
The Legacy
The Witches of Nakashige
Vanished Away

# ABOUT THE AUTHOR

I Talk You Talk Press is a Japan-based publisher of language textbooks, graded readers and language learning/teaching resources.

Our team is made up of highly experienced language teachers and translators, who have all studied at least one additional language to an advanced level.

This experience enables us to design our materials from the perspective of both the teacher and the learner. We consult with both teachers and language learners when designing our textbooks and graded readers, and test our materials extensively in the classroom before publication.

We are a fast-growing press, and currently publish graded readers for learners of English. We publish new graded readers monthly.

www.ingramcontent.com/pod-product-compliance
Lightning Source LLC
Chambersburg PA
CBHW022343040426

42449CB00006B/696